AF255456

Anger Management

How to Take Control of Your Emotions

Maxwell Donaldson

Contents

Introduction

Now before we understand the meaning of anger management, we need to know that the concept is rather simple. We are aiming to create fewer problem for ourselves.

Dealing with anger becomes easier when we are aware of its impact on our lives. How can we manage anger when we are unaware of its meaning?

Anger refers to the state of mind when we lack critical thinking. Some situations put our thinking capabilities to a halt and compel us to take irrational steps. This may come as a result of quarrels with a stranger, friends, a roommate, or even a spouse.

The intensity of anger varies. In some situations, we say harsh words while in others, we tend to be physically expressive. Both have equal implications. But what if you remain silent? This is not easy to achieve at first, but if you do, you become a beast. Period.

People who are hired for public positions tend to have more experience in handling anger situations whether they are sales staff or executives running an organization. Yes, besides hard skills and technical knowledge, there are soft skills that guarantee your job, and "anger Management" plays a vital role in confirming your position.

Understanding Anger

Understanding anger isn't the hard part. It refers to the burst of emotions that comes with a feeling of being low and not having control over your actions. This plays a key role in the destruction of any sensible person as they can fall into the trap where people put them.

Anger brings emotions into one's life and can destroy everything you are putting forth. Take this example; you are working and your boss calls you into his office. Due to your negligence, you have made a mistake for which boss screams at you, but you stand there without uttering a word. You understanding that you haven't done this thing, right. So, anger hits you.

Now you are on the street and suddenly hit from back by a biker, which is purely his mistake, so how you will respond? Being a gentleman, you will let this go, but what it is your mistake and he blames you. You will become angry. This is very normal.

Compare both examples side by side. In the first situation, you made a mistake and had done something wrong, yet you didn't get angry even after suffering humiliation and the degrading of your self-respect. Whereas in the second case, the mistake wasn't someone else's. That didn't hurt you, but still you got angry.

Therefore, it is better to understand that anger only comes from someone else's behavior, not yours. Even then, everyone says that anger isn't right!! While technically it is justified, in this state of mind, you are transferring something bad done to you to someone else.

Your boss gets angry at you, while you transferred it to the biker. Related things? Anger not only affects the person absorbing it but also creates a never-ending chain of bad vibes that are good for nothing.

An angry person sometimes reveals things meant to be secretively, resulting in handing power over the other person. Now, we have understood the meaning of anger so let's dive into the effects of anger on your life from every perspective.

Notes

____

____

____

____

____

____

____

____

____

____

Effects of Anger

Anger has devastating effects on many aspects important in your life. I will divide these things into a simplified list to help you better understand the consequences of anger.

Physical Health

Anger has a drastic effect on physical health. It can increase blood pressure, the level of cholesterol, and heart rate, causing various body malfunctions, angina, brain stress, and much more.

Sometimes, we ignore the fact that physical health is not only related to diseases, but this is not true. Occasionally, we fall into a health issue like not eating well, having poor at concentration, poor technical skills, and a reduction in judgment.

For this reason, it is always suggested to keep our anger on the low side, even when we are faced with a difficult situation. As per a recent survey by the English school of Arts, anger can cause 23% of your overall health problems that may manifest during the later stages of our lives when most of the organs and body muscles fail to cooperate, causing neural damage or worse.

Mental Health

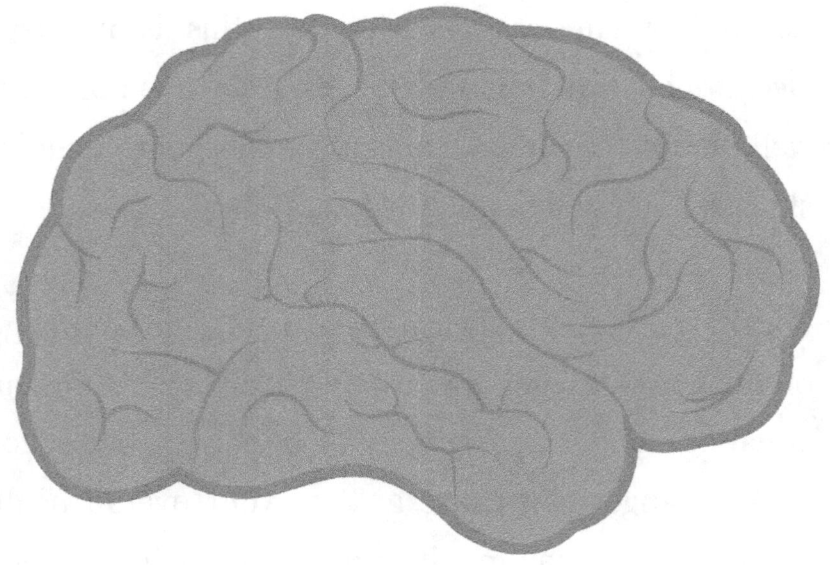

What is the actual meaning of mental health? We have touched on this point in physical health, as anger affects your mental health in such a way that you lose control over your life. Your personal life includes your parents, partner, children, and friends. You fail to respond appropriately to situations, which as a result creates a huge imbalance in your life.

A recent study by Harvard found that 34 out of 100 men and 26 out of 100 females have suffered from mental health problems at some point. This ultimately affected their lives in the negative, and according to some studies, people get so frustrated that they isolate themselves.

Careers

Have you ever imagined facing an angry student as a teacher or an angry boss as an employee? What impacts do they create on your life after an event? Take the perspective of a person who is very nice to everyone but gets hurts every time he is a victim of someone else's bad temper. Does his work efficiency increase or decrease?

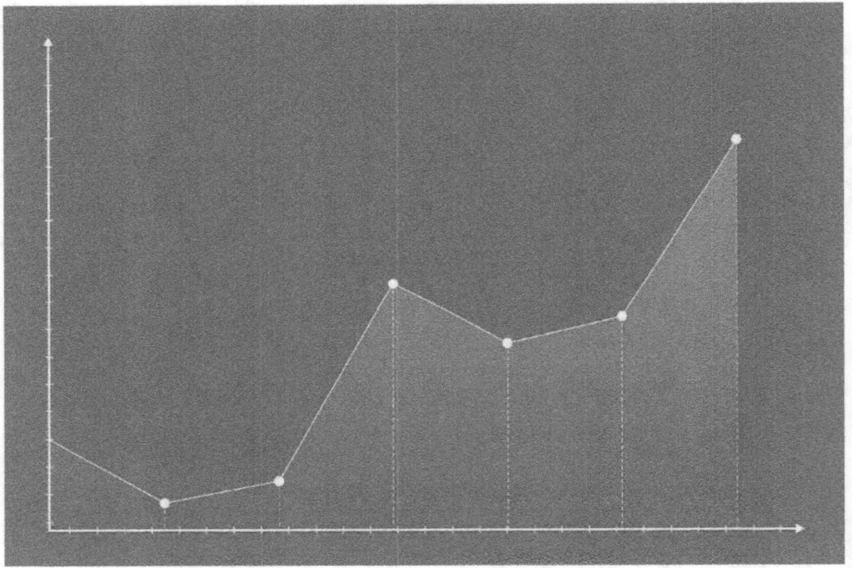

The impact on the teacher's performance and the aftermath for the worker after being humiliated by his boss in the work environment can be dire.

Anger not only decreases performance and affects one's career, but it can also create an atmosphere of revenge irrespective of the position held. This kills productivity and an encouraging environment. In some cases, the angry person might forget his behavior, but the second person remembers it and thinks of doing harm.

Relationships

We have often witnessed that the major cause of divorce and departure is anger or a short-tempered male or female. Relationships are made of mutual respect and honor such that the anger can shatter everything you have been building. Anger tarnished relationships even if it is just an outburst of a feeling.

Yet, it is understandable that in daily life, many things provoke anger. What if one partner is mad and angry at another, and the other remains calm and quiet instead of replying? The person who is at fault will realize his or her mistake. Not only this will prevent any misfortune, but it will also increase the level of respect and love.

So, what is required of you is to be silent and let the anger pass. Soon, everything will come to rest, and you will be in a better place than before.

Notes

Myth and Facts about Anger

Here comes the interesting part about anger... There are many myths and facts that needs to be addressed before you think it is natural and common.

The biggest myth surrounding anger says that it comes from people with whom you have personal attachments like family members and friends. This is not true. The fact is a wave of anger is not good nor bad, just anger.

Another myth states that anger only comes when you are dealing with a person at a lower level than you, like a janitor or worker. Such people may express their frustrations and anger without considering the impact it may impose on others' lives.

When you are in an anger situation with your employee or boss, should you quench your defense and take the blame and humiliation with a smile. Is this hypocrisy? Most people tend to take the stance that they can't bear anything said against them, and their anger is often difficult to control.

I have a question for them...What happens to this temper when facing someone of a higher financial status or position than yours? What happens when you are at a public gathering with public officials?

Think about it, and you will get the answer. Being humble and polite to everyone is necessary. The point is not to make you express bad behavior to higher authorities but to amend your behavior with people lower in status than you.

Restraint should be implemented in any case. Being nice and humble will not depreciate your self-importance and self-worth; rather it will demarcate you as a special person and role model.

Notes

____

____

____

____

____

____

____

____

____

How Anger Management Can Help

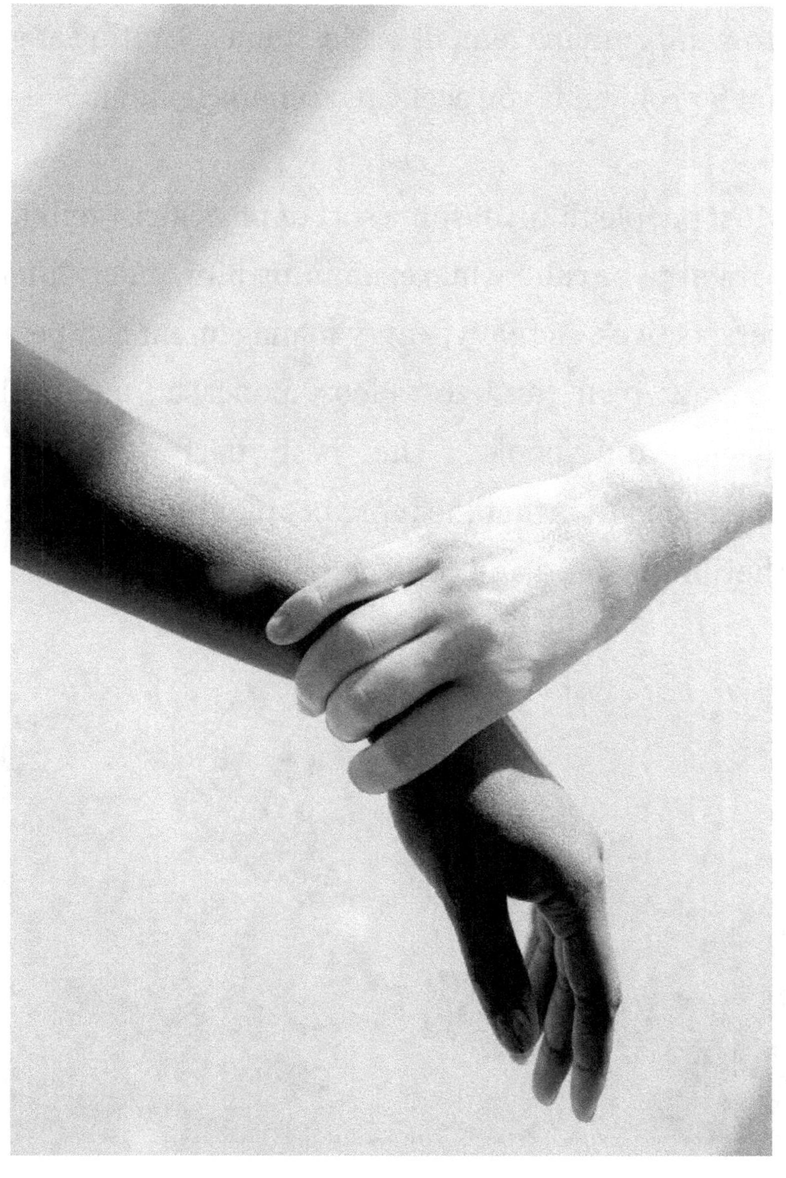

Being angry is quite common for most people nowadays, but we shouldn't shy away from getting help from anger management professionals. Getting angry is not a problem if you seek anger management.

Most people think of some sort of physiatrist telling the patient to be calm while examining him under different perspectives. Actually, angry management can be done on your own through videos, podcasts, audio clips, music, and books. The best part about anger management is that the more people study, it the better they understand and control the situation.

In the past, anger management was done in churches and temples in a session of peace and solitude for the fierce warriors. But now things have changed. Our lifestyles have changed and those old school methods are no longer effective.

Today, we mostly rely on print and digital media to cure people of the anger disease. Yes this can be called a disease as it dissolves a person mentally and psychologically. Anger management can help you get control over your nerves to remain calm in difficult situations.

You tend to think more rationally under pressure. You can learn the art of subjective criticism. Moreover, anger management is the only way to get back your life without compromising.

With this, I k now you can become a better version of yourself and enjoy the many rewarding results that only a person who has been through the process can have.

Notes

____

____

____

____

____

____

____

____

Reasons Behind Anger

The reasons behind anger are many. Let's divide them into different situation that affect a person's emotions that lead to angry behavior. In the work environment, it is very common to get angry due to the behavior of the boss, your colleagues, and even other workers you encounter.

Getting angry with your employee is very common nowadays. The main reason is that you don't get the work done in the right manner. Now, tell me what would you do if you were in the position of your boss? We generally think about things from a distance; all we need is to put ourselves in someone's shoes.

The situation can be avoided by doing the work correctly in the first place. In all fairness, you are being paid for the work you are doing; therefore, you have to perform as per expectations.

Now let's assume that you did everything right but still your boss gets angry at you. The main reason is a lack of communication skills, which you need to work on. Getting angry is not the solution. We have to look for the solution to avoid the anger, while improving ourselves. Isn't that better?

Now comes anger with your friends and colleagues. Talking about friends, they have been with you through thick and thin. They might have guided well to this point in your life. It is understandable that you had some argument with a friend and sometimes were harsh and aggressive.

Is this is what they should expect from you as a friend? Your friends are the most precious thing in the world, so losing them in a small quarrel isn't an option. Sometimes they are intentionally teasing you for fun. Bear that in mind and think for a while if just some fun is humiliating you in front of others or you are hurting yourself? (which isn't often the case). Then let it go and enjoy being with them.

Getting angry with colleagues is very common and is in many situations justified. The reason is that we all know in the cooperate world that everyone is competing to get the best of a situation. It is understandable, but this isn't always the case.

Colleagues are your friends and sometimes they spend more time with you compared to others, so they understand you better. Therefore, we have to respect the time and effort they put forth on our behalf.

And last comes the worker in the organization where you work or other people you came across. Getting angry generally comes with no real reason. Maybe you thought it might affect your self-respect or ego. This is the case when you think of yourself above people and you take pride in being who you are. You have done right for yourself, why should others bear your wrath?

The answer is no. These workers may be are very stressed out have other important things to deal with rather than you and your self-respect. Therefore, the takeaway here is that you should be patient and understand the situation and react by letting the little things go. It will be more beneficial for you and the other person too.

Notes

Anger Symptoms and How to Express Them

There are many symptoms of anger to be aware of before you consider yourself a complete person. Getting angry is not bad; what is bad that you are unaware of your behavior. I will divide this into different sections to help you better understand what is at stake.

Anger Triggers

This is the best and most common way to understand your anger. It will a very short and fun rehearsal. Just sit down and think about your present situation. If you feel you are not fine, postpone this activity to another time when you are feeling better. Now, take a notebook and write down every hour you spend in your day when anger or a strong feeling reared its ugly head.

After you have written down the time frame and respective feelings, next I want you to write the reason for each incident of strong feeling. After writing all the reasons, look back and observe any common behaviors or situations. The more you find the common problem, the more you will understand that these are anger triggers for you.

What Makes me Angry?

Now you have to ask a basic question: is the feeling associated with the anger? You may think that all the things that make you angry are the actual reasons for being angry. The situation becomes worse when you try to express the feeling in a more ferocious style.

Now that you have noted down what makes you angry, have a look at them and think of alternatives with different consequences of your actions and they would affect your life. You will better understand what makes you angry.

What do I Think?

Next, you want to consider is what you were thinking at that particular anger moment. Was it a strong feeling that lasted for the whole day. If that feeling was temporary, then it is not an exaggerated form of anger. Maybe it is just a grudge against someone, which is even more dangerous than anger. Therefore, look around for the reasons that make you feel angry and try to correct them by thinking of alternatives.

Keeping Calm

Being calm at the time of anger isn't always possible. Most people express their anger in the form of insulting or abusing others, even in front of other people. The option of being calm is not generally considered when we think of abrupt situations where anger lingers.

To remain calm, we have to think positively. For example, we have to assume that another person might be experiencing something bad in his life. We have to come up with positive and insightful reasoning so we can calm ourselves and remain steadfast in this inner peace.

Developing a Solution

Tell me about a time when you had to look for a solution to your anger. Instead of focusing on the solution, we humans as a rule try to circle the problem, which the problem worse. Coming up with a solution with a thoughtful mind is very important to control anger.

The task is quite simple: you just have to highlight the reasoning behind the cause of your anger and relate it to a possible solution. The best solution is not possible at the moment but later you can search for it. This is because controlling anger is not a one-time process; it takes time to be a better person. When you find a solution, note it down because this way for a future similar situation.

The Beginning of Change

If you control your anger, you can bring change in your life. It has an incremental effect over time. The beginning of change is not just controlling your anger but when first realizing a personality defect.

Let me give you a perspective. Your practical life, your personal life, and your work life will improve substantially. You will no longer be affected by the sarcasm. You can joke with your friends and, most importantly, you will handle minor quarrels with your spouse more intelligently.

Notes

Healthy Ways of Controlling Anger

Have you ever thought of healthy ways to control your anger? Controlling anger is not a checklist of bullet points; rather, anger is controlled by some health-related actions.

The best way you can control your anger is to stay calm and composed and look for the alternatives to improve the situation and prevent matters from getting worse. Think at the brighter side of things and remember the good deeds the person has done for you in the past. We have to understand that the other person might not have done something intentionally or he might be making fun with you, not of you.

When you think you are getting angry, just sit down where you are and keep silent. Have a glass of water because according to a study by a Harvard team, anger can be suppressed by just a glass of water. Therefore, when you feel angry, take a glass of water and assume with every sip that you are taking in the anger and depressing it.

The best you can do at the time of anger is to remain silent. This will not only improve the situation, but it will compel the other person to think about his action. In some cases, he might even excuse you. If not, ask for the reason behind their anger. This will not only create an atmosphere of friendliness, but also it will give you clues about your personality defect so you can remedy it.

The last thing you can do is to say okay and move on. Or explain your point a way they can understand their misunderstanding. The study revealed that when you agree with the other person's point of view, they lay down a wall of acceptance, and you are in a better position to rationally accept their mistake.

Notes

Benefits of Using Humor

The best and most effective form of anger management is the use of humor. Humor can not only be used to limit anger, but it is sometimes utilized to get rid of an old habit. We have seen several cases in which anger was diverted with the use of humor. By humor, we don't mean making jokes in a serious situation; rather, we can foster a smile in the other person.

Humor has been used for centuries to get rid of anger. This technique was likely used in old Hindu temples to combat pain and misery. From studies, it has been proven that humor creates a sense of admiration and acceptance for the person using it. Humor has been seen as a driving force create self-satisfaction and a feeling of welcomeness. Listen to people's minds first to avoid anger circumstances that create panic instead of wellness.

Use Professional Help

We can use professionally help to get rid of our anger. Anger management techniques are very fruitful and each person learns to handle his case. Some people think of psychiatrist as a rip off, but know that they can help through anger management by setting up a good routine so you can be calm and productive.

There are circumstances in which professional is needed to deal with mental issues - not to mention physical ones, as they are often psychological. Recent studies show that ordinary persons cannot avail themselves of this opportunity; but when they can, professional help require a great amount of care and time. If the fees are too great, there may be alternatives such as pro bono services.

The professionals have provided a breakthrough in anger management. These healthcare professionals are trained to transform people according to their individual needs. The best part about this profession is the new gain in knowledge.

Many passionate people chose to enter this exciting field. Why not try this approach rather than flounder in your anger and get worse.

Each patient has their hot points. The psychologist or psychiatrist not only monitors their anger but also take a close look at the physical aspects of their behavior. Therefore, you can your money to get results without worry.

Notes

Managing Children and Young People

Managing children and young people is not easy as they are full of energy and active behavior. They are not always rational. It has been observed that every 6 out of 10 children in the US is short-tempered and angry at even small things. Parents have to spend quite a bit of time with them.

There is a huge misconception about dealing with the younger generation. They are often taught by their teachers and parents to be straightforward with unknown people. Yes, you have to be straightforward with strangers, but that doesn't mean you have to the impolite and with relatives and friends.

Therefore, parents and teachers must talk to their children and tell them about manners and ethics. They should be given a way to interact with new people so they can understand different perspectives. Parents can go one step further by guiding them, using books or showing them insightful documentaries to help them grasp the knowledge correctly.

Notes

Working with Angry Children

We sometimes came across children who are very aggressive and need proper anger management to excel in their careers. Working with angry children is often very difficult as they tend not to understand it at first. The problem is that tend to get hyper and express their feelings aggressively.

Some are introverted and live in a separate world in their minds. Parents need to be very cautious about the behavior of these kids and have to remove any barrier to understanding. These kids require special attention, but they can learn very easily if guided properly.

We have seen occasions where teachers find it very difficult to deal with their aggressive students. The teacher has a lot of responsibilities but should avoid talking loudly or shouting at them and instead of using politeness. Sometimes they need to use strictness, but there should be a proper balance to carry out learning.

Tips for Parents of Toddlers

Occasionally, it is possible to find a toddler suffering from anger management issues. At a very young age, they rely on outbursts to express themselves. The major issue is the attitude of the parents and a mutual non-understanding. Therefore, parents have huge responsibility to bring these kids to a quiet state.

As toddlers don't go to school, especially the mother has the main responsibility to build self-worth in the child. Toddlers have to be taken seriously and may be given serious talks.

Tips for Parents of Teenagers

Most anger management issues of teenagers exist because they are in a rapid growing stage and need proper care from parents and teachers alike. This is the age that can make or break their adult lives; therefore, we have to be very vigilant. At this growing age, teen get a lot of information from everywhere around, making them impatient with their parents as a source of knowledge.

Generally, these are the inherited issues or they have seen anger at home. Proper classes and lectures given to these special kids can help. The teacher will usually treat every student equally but some need more help. They look grown up but can use the same amount of attention as a toddler. Parents have to understand that a teenager is not an adult; just a grown toddler.

In most countries, teenage anger management classes have been started. They are becoming very helpful for parents and for teachers in controlling angry kids. Separate lesson plans decrease barriers and increase effective communication.

Notes

The Nature of Anger

We usually think that getting upset or frustrated by the harsh word of others is bad. This is not the case. In reality, this has a very close relationship with how we react in general in our personal lives.

We used to think of anger symptoms as objective but they have proved to be subjective. This means that every person put into the same situation will react differently.

The best way to cognitively check the person's pattern is by observing the nature of their anger. You have to keep a very close eye on the effects of their behavior. We can maintain a precise record of actions and reactions.

Then we will see that the nature of anger varies in different situations. You might be thinking how I can check the nature of the anger or the sensitivity of the subject? This is a very interesting question. The best way is to observe your friends, colleagues, working staff, or maybe your boss and observe them and compare their reactions.

You will find out that the nature of these response will be different than yours. Then you will compare what was right and what was wrong. You may find that sometimes you just overreact to simple situations rather than being calm and composed. You must learn to let go instead of getting angry.

Notes

Expressing Anger

You know that expressing anger can be very important to mental health rather than keeping silent. One time I say I have to be silent, while now I am saying that I have to be expressive? What does this mean?

According to some research, some people find it very difficult to control themselves and remain silent and instead of continuously waiting for the moment to explode. In this scenario, expressing anger in the right manner is very important because when you do nothing, you are thinking about getting revenge.

This proves to be very counterproductive and may lead to depression and anxiety. So how best can we express our anger? We have seen in movies that some angry people bang their head on the desks or hit the walls with their fits, but that is not the case in reality. What you can do to express your anger is talk to a very close friend. A friend can understand without saying a word. You can pour your heart out without worrying about the consequences.

Some research has found that the best way you can express your anger is to write down your feelings. This not only shaping your anger in the right manner, but it is also a record to go back to when in anger to help you think more rationally about what you could have done differently.

Another way is to a colleague and express your feelings. The best part about friends and colleagues is that they are so close to you that they sometimes understand your feelings without saying a word.

Of course, a friend or colleague can be pushed to the wall. Plus, they might have been in the same situation at one time.

Why are Some People Angrier than Others?

We have witnessed many people get angrier than a normal person. What is the actual reason behind it? Recent studies show that temper and anger are very closely related to where and how you are raised. Sometimes, people are raised in a very tense environment, and they remain stressed in similar circumstances later. That doesn't mean they have no tolerance at all, but their level of tolerance is very low as compared to other people.

This is about the relationship you had with your parents. There are different situations like your parents got divorced or separated; maybe you are sent to boarding school at a very young age; you were a victim of child abuse; your family members were not supportive, you faced betrayal from your friends, or the person you loved left.

This does not end here as according to some research, around 30% of actual domestic problems occurred prior? To make things more interesting, it was found that parents' personal relationship impacts up to 90% of the child's future life. Which bring us to the conclusion that it doesn't matter if your parents are scientists, philosophers or doctors. If they have personal issues, it can bring harm to the life of their child.

If parents are having problems with each other, they will have to communicate with their kid. Parents try to put a new spin on obvious things, and the kid understands it only too well. Before familial tension affects the child's development, you have to intervene and explain the situation in the best possible manner so the child can react properly.

Relaxation

It is observed that the main cause of anger is due to restlessness and depression, or maybe anxiety. The best possible remedy is to relax and spend time with your family, friends, or anyone you care about.

We can be so entrenched in our work that we forget to spare time for ourselves, which is very dangerous as we are burning the candle at both ends, bringing on more problems. Relaxation is very important and should be practiced every day - and not on weekends only.
You don't have to be always working on something after working hours because that is the time to give yourself. Think about the hobbies and give yourself a break. The best part about hobbies is that they can be used to supplement your income, but they can also drive your attention away from work.

You can get a double benefit by having a hobby like fishing that you can parlay into something else. You can write a book if you are an expert or maybe start a new business selling fishing gear.

Therefore this hobby not only brings you joy, but it also helps you achieve something bigger in the long run. Obviously, you don't have to do fishing as a hobby as there are numerous hobbies on the internet or they can come from your friends.

So getting time out, having some new hobbies, and spending time with your family are all very important. We sometimes think that productive time is only when we are doing something. When we get home from work, we scroll through Facebook for half an hour and think that we have whiled away our time.

We forget to understand that we have devoted that time to ourselves, and we don't have to be productive every moment of every day. We just have to do things that make us happy rather than rich.

Cognitive Restructuring

You might be thinking, what is the meaning of cognitive restructuring? This is a process in which you realize your actions and reactions to correct them in the future. So what that mean? Cognitive restructuring comes from using several parameters.

Those parameters are defined subjectively, and they cannot be applied to people with different thoughts and backgrounds. Some factors that create differences are money, favor, power, and value.

Every person has their own set of requirements for self-fulfillment. Compare a CEO to a janitor. Their jobs and work requirements are a hundred and eighty degrees part, which means that their cognitive restructuring would be different.

The janitor might compromise on self-respect, bearing in mind that he could get fired. But the CEO will have a different set of values upon which his life revolves. Most likely, he prioritizes his self-respect before anything else.

So cognitive restructuring is very important as it can help an individual to think logically and respond according to the situation at hand in a manner that will help in the future.

Notes

____

____

____

____

____

____

____

____

____

____

Better Communication

We should talk about the importance of good communication skills for every walk of life, but anger management communication plays a critical role be it with a friend, colleague, or maybe a spouse. The best road to anger management is better communication. It should decrease stress by helping you think in a more positive fashion.

Sometimes we are in situations in which we cannot communicate properly. We may have private problems with our friends, our spouses, or our parents. We should be in a better position to share our feelings and get some valuable feedback.

Some of you might come across people who seem more comfortable in sharing their problems with anger management professionals. This is because these professionals are highly trained and skillful compared to the other people in your life. This may come at some cost to you, but they are usually very helpful.

Changing your Environment

Talking about the importance of the environment, we need to express ourselves and remain resilient in crucial times. We have to ask a question, are we in the right environment?

The right environment could be ay home, with our neighbors, a group of friends or colleagues. What does the environment matter. The answer is we have to consider it when we are cognitive restructuring our anger issues.

These are additional factors like our jobs. The question is: is this job right for me? Am I justifying my capabilities and career goals? Where will I be in the next five years? By asking these questions, you will eventually conclude that you are either in the right place or not.

A major question I get is why are we on this earth? Is it to become competent and achieve something to avoid depression and anxiety. You are procrastinating every time you open your laptop. You see your goals revolving around you, but you don't do anything about them other than looking at them hopelessly.

On the other hand, if you are very happy with your current situation, anger and procrastination will fade away. You will be more happy with your life and eventually, the anger management issue is resolved. You are likely in the right location and at the right time. No more analyzing as you are very good where you are.

Now what should we do? Instead of an anger management professional, you could consult a career management professional who will guide your upcoming life. You could look around for new job opportunities, or if you are confident enough, you can ask for raise. If that is not possible, start thinking about your own business because that is going to be a lot more lucrative down the road.

Methods

Do you know that you can control your anger by following a predetermined method used by professionals? You know that anger is subjective; therefore each method has its effectiveness.

Recently it was discovered that many factors play a crucial role in maintaining the daily life of most people. You might have temper issues and none seem relevant. But the answer is each factor self-explanatory, and you just have to apply them when you are not feeling good, rather than learning or decoding some programming language. These methods are:

Countdown

Ever think that a countdown could be an effective way of controlling your anger? This technique was used by monks and priests to help people getting over anger. The concept is very simple: when you are not feeling good, you just start doing a countdown without letting the other person know you are counting.

Some urge that we should have a countdown goal in our minds. But this depends on the person, his mental stability and how he incorporates the method in a given situation. You can count fast you can count slow: it doesn't matter because the concept is that when you start counting, you are helping your mind deviate from something that makes you angry that keeps circling again and again.

This method is not only helpful in getting around issues, but it also is very helpful in fighting depression and anxiety. This technique is also used by people who teach the hyper focus concept, or the importance of focusing on one thing at a particular time. The rehearsal goes like this: you start doing a countdown when you are feeling anger, while keeping in mind that when you reach the end of the countdown, you assume your anger is gone.

If after the countdown, you are still feeling angry, you have assure yourself that you are no longer angry at all. The beautiful part of this method is that even if you are angry, it will help you maintain your decorum. Utilizing this concept is purely dependent on you and how you make it effective and self-sustaining.

Take a Breather

Have you ever thought of taking a long breath when in anger? This method is generally followed by monks when they are chanting or focusing. If we take the help of science, we will come to realize that when you take a long breath, you are getting the proper oxygen. This way your organs are respiring at their best, helping you control your emotions.

Following the pattern of taking long breaths is not very difficult; moreover it also helps you in speaking more confidently and deeply. Pretend you are feeling normal and take a proper breath. This is scientifically proven to help those suffering from mental illness. Any science geek out there should love this concept.

In the practical world, the effects can be replicated by keeping away from a bad situation and taking a long breath. So if you are in the office, go to the washroom or parking area where no one is around. It is always recommended to go to a place where there is a lawn or pond. You are away from the situation and that anger feeling when start taking the long breath.

When you take a breath of fresh air, you are taking in positivity and goodwill, thereby removing the bad from your body. You have to remind yourself of all the positive and helpful situations of your life, so you can let go. The best part about this technique is that it can be replicated by anyone at any time and any place.

Go Walk Around

Getting away from the situation where your anger is aroused is not running away from facing things; in reality, it is helping you finding a way to get rid of negativity.

This purely depends on the circumstances. If you are in direct communication with someone, obviously you cannot leave the conversation to go for a walk. Rather, when you are alone and thinking of the situation again. this is the time to reflect.

The implementation of this concept is common and very easy as you just have to leave the situation. What happens if you are in a meeting? Well, in the first place, you should get angry in a meeting. So what if your boss is specifically pointing at you for your poor performance. But if you can excuse yourself to go to the washroom, do so to calm down, and take your time.

It's a lot easier when you are alone in your office; then you can take a walk or go to the lounge.

Repeat a Mantra

If you have attended a yoga class, you might already know this concept and the effectiveness it possesses. The concept of a mantra is itself not difficult to comprehend. In fact, it can be used by anyone if they understand its implementation.

From the technical perspective, you are repeating a word again and again to clear your mind. This proven technique is best done alone, although groups can do it as well. Sometimes you have to repeat the words in the loud voice which might disturb others.

The implementation of a mantra is very simple if you use a powerful word that is relevant to you. There has been a long debate over which words to repeat to be motivational or emotional, but the point of discussion is that you must repeat it. Some examples are names, foreign words, or feeling words like love, honesty, honor, or caring.

You might be thinking how can emotional words help in a mantra? Emotional words can help in most any scenario. Imaging controlling a situation that might have eventually lost your job and as a result, your family suffered. Instead, it is time to develop an emotional balance.

The mantra technique requires that you either say the word or words aloud or in your heart? This is purely dependent on you. Over time, you can apply it at will any time. But if you are the sort of person who finds it difficult to concentrate, you have to repeat the mantra in a louder voice, requiring personal isolation.

Stretching

Stretches can help in anger management? When you are doing physical exercise, you are helping your body to release a hormone or endorphin that will cause mental satisfaction and achieving hyper focus.

Mental classes using this concept when you are stressed, depressed or anxious. But can it be effective in dealing with anger? When you are stretching, you are using all your body muscles to respond in one particular fashion. Your brain gets overloaded with physical stimuli, thereby decreasing negative thought and desires.

You don't have to go above and beyond; just a few simple exercises will do the work. You don't have to spend a considerable amount of your time or be in a gym because stretching is just relaxing your muscles rather than putting a load on them and depriving them of oxygen, creating tiredness and drowsiness.

Some handbooks mentioned that stretching means taking a hot shower, which is very helpful to relax the muscles and the mind. However, you can stretch while making your coffee, arranging your files, or reaching to something. Over time you will feel the great benefit of it.

Mental Escape

Mental escape means walking away from a bad situation and becoming unconscious of your environment. It enables you to be carefree and mentally stable.

Escapism has been touted by renowned scholars and teachers to uplift the morale and motivation of their students. Some experience extreme amounts of stress and anxiety. The major concern is to ensure that anger issues don't impact our mental health. Then the remedy is quite different.

You can speak your heart to a friend as a form of mental escape or maybe you can consult a professional. We have to understand that whether escape is achieved or accomplished is the point alone or with someone else. Say you get home after a tiring day at work; talking to your spouse can be a mental escape. But it doesn't mean leaving things completely aside, but it means adopting the more fruitful and rewarding topics.

We have to make sure that we are helping ourselves and not escaping from the situation we are in. Say, you go on a walk on the beach or take a sun bath. These are sources of mental escape that can help you ease your nerves and break the shackles of unhappiness and boredom.

Sometimes talking to someone can provide mental escape whereas a quarrel will only increase your stress. I have observed on several occasions that a person who needs mental escape seeks out the wrong choice. When things back fire, they avoid people to get some rest. This is not a way to get some self-help.

To get a mental escape, no need to spend thousands on a short time remedy. Rather celebrate someone's success and give them your blessing. Get out of yourself and inner focus. Imagine the love you will get in response from that person, their family, and their social circle. Mental escape is truly related to your good deeds and their effect on others; it will impact your life and provide you with unmatchable mental freedom.

Stop Talking

When we think of anger management, it could entail stopping to talk with the people irritating us. It may seem unwise, but there may be no other choice to avoid amental collapse.

The biggest issue faced by most people is that they react way too early without considering the situation. We have to be patient and remain silent for a time. You will get to voice your side of the issue, but be mindful whether the time is right for discussion or not.

Coping with anger management issues means a concern for their impact on other people's life. Sometimes we think that presenting our side of the story will clear the air and make the situation better. To the contrary, talking can worsen the situation. The most important factor revealed by basic science is that speak before acting rationally when angry.

When we try to over explain a situation, it can be very concerning to the other person. It takes tact to get good results. If you are experiencing bad feelings inside and the person is really burning you up, speak from your heart.

I have seen people hide their feeling and emit a fake acknowledgment that does not ring true.. The best thing at the time of anger is to remain quiet and let the things cool down. Wait until you can be logical and use a calm tone. There is no need to cut the other person down and create more negative feelings that can affect the relationship in the future. Think before you speak, or don't speak at all.

Take a Timeout

The best part about anger management is that it can help you take time out and spend it on better matters. Normally, we are preoccupied in our day-to-day lives that we avoid taking time for ourselves and our family, which affects our performance and productivity.

We have to take time to think more logically and give our best to others. Stress, anxiety, and depression sometimes lead to irrational behavior and anger. Too much work and other people's problems take their toll.

Most of us are driven by the lust for money, and as a result, we forgot to take time for ourselves and what is really important for our spiritual wellbeing. Taking time out doesn't mean that you have to leave everything and go on a month-long leave; it means letting go of the thing circling our minds.

You don't have to be a monk and go to China to spend your rest of the life in peace, doing yoga; but instead, you have to be living in this world, experiencing day-to-day life. Why do we keep on doing the wrong things again and again that disrupt our minds and deprive us of critical thinking.

The best to avoid this perennial situation is to write down on a piece of paper what is disturbing you and paste it on a whiteboard or even your wall. This makes your anger emotions real and also reminds you that you worried about a problem, which is not a problem at all. Our mind is trained to mull over problems that jam it up. Therefore the best practice is to let things go and opt for the best scenario.

Laughter

The best lesson in anger management is laughter. It has been professionally proven that laughing can bring joy in your life and its surroundings and diminish stress and anxiety.

Laughing not only creates a sense of happiness, but it also creates an environment of positivity that other people can feel. Laughing can improve a tense situation and decrease the chance of a quarrel arising between two people. Sometimes we are in a critical situation, where we have to be vigilant and remain silent. We are with a friend and some issue occur, forcing us to cool down. Humor and laughter can save the day.

Laughing not only improves the situation but also elevate the status you may hold in the eyes of another person. It could lead to a good ending and even improve the relation between you and the other person.

I don't mean that you have to be a jerk or a clown. A simple smile can do wonders. Sometimes laughing loudly worsens the situation because other people might not be interested in your humor at the moment. Therefore, you have to be very careful in choosing this path as it may aggravate conflicts as well.

Imagine Forgiving

Have you ever thought of forgiving a person who is the cause of your anger? The biggest problem is that we tend to live with our feelings and often associate a particular person with them. We may as a result develop a grudge and want to take revenge, so we wait for the best time to come.

The bad part about revenge it deprives you of critical thinking and rational analysis, affecting your productivity and your life because it consumes you. Have you ever thought about the result of letting things go? Maybe that person will think you have surrendered, while in reality, you have won.

Revenge compels you to look at everything from a skewed angle. It can only lead to harming yourself and/or another. That path will be damaging to ourselves first and foremost. The reality is that we have to live with the situation. Are women more likely than man to plot revenge. Now that is an unproved and controversial question, but it lingers nonetheless.

Looking for the opportunity to extend forgiveness is fruitful and rewarding. Forgiving will create an environment of friendliness and care for other people. People who can forgive know they are doing the right thing. In the end, it is always advisable to forgive even guilty people because you don't know where they are coming from. The best you can do is to put yourself in their shoes and decide to let go.

Sleeping Well

Getting the best sleep is very important in controlling behavior. You may have found that sometimes we are under a lot of stress and tired due to even routine chores, and as result of sleeplessness, we are compelled to take irrational steps.

According to research, you need at least 7 to 8 hours of sleep daily. Non-spontaneous irregular sleep, such as napping, is not good for your health as it increases body part efficiency. The best we can do is to get at least 6 hours of sleep as a regular pattern and without any disturbance.

When you are not getting proper sleep, emotional control is difficult. A lack of sleep exacerbates other ailments. Insomnia from cell phones, laptops and other digital devices before bed wreaks havoc on one's health. It is wise to cut down on screen time at night, including TV.

Make a regular pattern of your sleep time. Good sleep impacts your productivity the next day. People have different work schedules so you set your own hours. Just follow the same routine. Sleeping not only affects your mood and emotions but also the working capacity of your organs and muscles.

Doing Exercise

I have talked about stretching, but exercise is different. By exercise, I mean going to the gym and doing some hard on your body to a point where you are sweaty and tired.

Sometimes we are so entrenched in our routines that we forget to exercise. We don't seem to have the time to even take a long walk. Among the many benefits of exercise, it increases your heart rate, decreases cholesterol, prevents anemia, and makes you healthy and slim, keeping obesity at bay. Other than food, it is how we put energy into our lives.

There are many articles on line and documentaries about fitness and exercise. You can follow a classes virtually or in person as part of your daily life. The experts say to get at least thirty minutes a day of vigorous workout. Find what suits your style.

You don't have to go too hard on your body which may result in injuries. If you have shoulder problems, heavy weights are not suggested. You might opt for the treadmill or bench press, or even little dumbbells. The gym is full of choices. Gt a trainer if in doubt.

Exercise can help you blow off steam if you need anger management. Maybe you do exercise as a habit or hobby. Anger management is a slow and continuous and slow process utilizing many techniques, and good sleep and exercise are certainly among them.

Motivational videos work wonders for athletes and sportsmen, and they can work for you. Experts k now that when you do frequent exercise, you can feel your energy rising, and it gets transformed into productive work. Our bodies adapt to circumstances. Doing a lot of exercise might seem tedious or boring, but given the results, you become motivated to continue on and make it a lifestyle.

According to some research, only 55% of adults exercise while only 28% of the elderly do. It is a major cause of chronic diseases. We consume a lot of protein in our diets and a lot of carbs and fat. We need a way to burn this fuel.

When you are not mentally and physically healthy, you can counter the issues of anger and bad habits like procrastination. Exercise brings out the best in everyone. It boosts confidence socially and at work. Confident people believe in their capabilities and want to show the world what they can do. This makes them special. You can achieve this by simply exercising on a regular basis.

Managing Stress Recap

Managing stress is important to one's personal and social life. As it is subjective, control varies from person to person. You can emotionally control by limiting interaction with others, avoiding toxic people, and dismissing negative thoughts. Staying silent is a form of interaction, however. The point is to manage stress and keep anger at bay.

You never want things to get bitter in a social exchange, with anyone be it family, colleagues or friends. Once the words are said, they are out in the open, and you can't retrieve them. All the more reason to stay in control. While expressing yourself is fine, there is a definite demarcation line between self-expression of emotions and anger.

You can manage stress by talking to a professional as discussed before. Professionals are not only well trained but they also possess very strong ethical values with a commitment to their patients.

The next thing you can do is to limit your interaction with toxic and negative people. You cannot avoid them, but it can direct your energy toward something more productive.

Most of the time, those close to you are aware of your situation. Good communication keeps you emotionally connected. You can get honest advice without being judged.

The point is that emotions are complex and variable in different people, but many have similar anger management issues. It is often the environment at home or work. The point is to recognize your patterns and work to change them.

Step Away

When it comes to very toxic people and situations, it can deplete your energy. It is easier said than done to stay away. Realize what they are doing to your confidence and self-image.

You need to step away from toxic people. Limit your exposure to them at the office by making excuses to avoid them. You are not only helping yourself but them. It minimizes their impact. You might be the target and removing it may calm their anger.

People have different backgrounds and problems that may create harshness in their tone. Some of the people we come across in life are in control of their behavior and they are honest and straightforward. Sorry to tell you that this is not always the case. Learn to accept people for who they are and you won't get so riled up next time someone crosses you. It is human nature.

Throughout our lives, we interact with with people: sometimes we have good experience and sometimes bad ones. Although we cannot avoid people, we can stay vigilant.

This is a long process and obviously takes time. it is recommended to avoid people that vex you and stir up emotions. It may be a personality conflict as we are all different in our tolerance level.

Manage Your Thoughts

Did you know that managing your thoughts is very difficult, but vital, when you are angry and not thinking logically. As yourself, how we can I manage my thoughts if I am not thinking rationally?

The best practice to manage bad thoughts is to remain silent. By remaining silent, you are not only controlling your thoughts but you are also limiting the negative aspects of your environment from affecting you. It is a way not to respond.

Forgiving is another way to manage bad thoughts, especially those toward others. Forgiving removes negative feelings for a person and turns them into positive ones, thereby helping both of you. Forgiving releases fruitful results and maintains a healthy environment.

Your thoughts can also be managed by keeping them in check. Staying mentally and physically fit fights stress, anxiety and depression. Feeling good helps you focus on the positive side of things and let the negativity go. While negativity is all too common, it can be dispelled with the right techniques. So don't' give up.

A good way to manage anger is to indulge in positive activities like a hobby. A hobby provides benefits like turning your attention away from anger issues and monotonous daily tasks. As a result, you can decrease your stress level and go in a more positive direction. When you have a hobby, you can enjoy yourself, irrespective of your current emotional level.

Good habits are like good hobbies; they are healthy and fruitful. It can be going to bed early, getting up early in the morning, reading helpful books, checking your mailbox regularly to stay in touch with friends, and avoiding the stress of other people. No need to get enmeshed in the worries of the world. Busy bodies generate tension and spread gossip. No one benefits.

Hobbies and habits take you away from stress. They help you enjoy a productive work and home environment. Why not temper your workload a bit with some exercise, a long walk, time at the gym or some sports.

Get Away

Anger management means getting away from the bad mood you are currently in. Most people say that getting away from the problem is not the solution, but it certainly is a mode of control.

You cannot always leave your family or workplace with repercussions, but you can walk away from a quarrel.

Getting away is not always easy as you have to cope with the wrath of those avoided later. But at the moment, you are out of the storm. Come back and talk to your friend or partner when everyone has calmed down. Winning an argument is not your job in life, nor will boost your reputation and self-respect. Stay out of trouble and forget your ego.

We get cocky if we think we have the answer to everything. We don't want to be on the losing side and have people think we have done something wrong. Good people will be fair. Nothing good comes from trying to be superman than just ourselves.

If you don't insist on winning all the time, people will back you and speak in your favor. Most want to celebrating your goodness. Be mindful of how valuable your closed circle is in maintaining your position in the world.

Explore Your Feelings

Exploring your feelings can help diagnose the causes of your anger to help you understand and fight it. Understanding leads to dealing effectively with things on an emotional level. The exploration of feelings plays a key role in anger management.

The best way to explore feelings is to take time to assess how you act during the whole day. Remind yourself of any bad actions that affected you and your performance – and that you regret. You can consult a friend who knows you well and can evaluate your behavior if you lack self-awareness.

Alone or with someone, learn the reasons for and symptoms of your anger so you don't continue bad patterns. Read articles and books specifically designed for self-help. Look for renowned authors and their recent findings. Psychology and anger management is an evolving field.

Your thoughts and actions can only be managed by you and you have to want to change. We have to be steadfast and determined to solve this problem.

Focus of Relaxation

Various schools of thought focus on relaxation as playing a vital role in anger management. By relaxation, we mean remaining calm yet resilient under certain circumstances.

You have to decide which method will work best for your anger management, but be sure to try relaxation. For example, when you arrive home after work and start watching your favorite TV show, you are winding down. Some people enjoy hanging out with friends to get relaxed. Every person has his or her way of gaining relaxation; therefore, there is no general rule for everyone to follow.

Nonetheless, relaxation increases productivity and one's effectiveness in the workplace. If you are relaxed, chances are you will avoid outbursts. It is not about escape or just rest. You will come to look forward to how much it helps your self-control and relationships with others..

Therapy

What is therapy? It is professional help. In the case of anger management, it can be specialized psychological reconditioning. There are many approaches as you have seen including using a mantra or repeated word to calm and clear the mind. A coach can help you learn this form of meditation. Other therapists concentrate on stress control and self-awareness exercises.

Other therapies advocate taking a long breath to provide the lungs with more oxygen to increase the performance of the muscles and organs. Improving our communication skills in therapy can help you get along better with others. Sometimes you have to learn to talk to different types of people in particular situations.

Keep an Anger Diary

It is time to acknowledge who you are and the degree of anger you generate. Anger can get the best of us when we least expect it. Do you know how often it arises? Do you evaluate the cause and consequence?

To know more about yourself and eventually take the right action, keep a diary of all the occasions when you got angry. When you arrive home after a day at the office, write down your whole day and think critically about your actions. Analyze what you have done right or wrong.

This is helpful because after an anger situation is gone your mind, you return to normal and forget about it. Read that diary from time to time. Maybe after a few months or even a year. Compare yourself then and now. If you have not made critical improvement, keep on working at anger management and reread this book. If you take it seriously, it will come to pass.

Find a Way to Express Anger

We have to find a way to express our anger as it is very important as our mental and physical health. Uncontrolled or unexpressed anger can burst forth unexpectedly. We sometimes think that keeping silent is the way to suppress anger and negative thoughts. While it is useful in some contexts, it is not always your best option. We have to express our anger positively lest it devour us and lead to feelings of revenge or worse.

Use the techniques in this book or get the help of a friend or colleague. Healthcare professionals and anger management coaches take pride in listening to their clients' problems. That can be the start of real progress. They will often suggest forgiveness when a grudge lingers too long. It is always advisable to have a person in your life who can hear all your problems without judging you. Then you can work on yourself on your own.

Focus on the Solution, not the Problem

Sometimes, we are stuck in a problem such that we only think about it and not the solution. We are by nature pessimists, and we tend to see things from a negative perspective.

We think that discussing our problems will solve them; in reality, it is the total opposite. Discussing ad infinitum will increase the problem, and we are left wondering why we are so distressed.

Entrepreneurs and businessmen know that solutions are the way to go and they are proactive. You will be always surrounded by problems at home or in the workplace, but if you come up with solutions, you can be a role model or even a hero.

This applies well to anger management in that you have to find the symptoms and causes for your behavior first before the best solution is at hand. Some things are not in your control, and you can do nothing about them. But some can be corrected. You have to look into what is possible and acknowledge anything letting you down to take charge of your mistakes.

Notes

____

____

____

____

____

____

____

____

Give Yourself Time

Give yourself time to decide between the different factors responsible for your anger. Ask yourself, what factors are adding to my sufferings? Sometimes, we think of the common generic causes in normal people and consider them to be our own symptoms of anger.

However, if there is some issue with your personality, then there is no shame in accepting it because it might be affecting your life and the people around you. Anger management is very problematic as it can disturb your personal and financial life very strongly. Therefore, you have to understand yourself and give time to understanding your problems and the best solutions among those offered here.

How are going to solve a problem if you are unaware of the problem? While it is not bad to be a mildly short tempered person, if you are unaware of your problem, it can multiply and grow into a major anger issue. Therefore, spend some time with an anger management professional to help you tackle the tough issues. Having finished this book, you are one of the lucky people who has come to understood their mental capacity because most people don't even get through stage one.

Notes

____

____

____

____

____

____

____

____

____

____

____

____

Focus on Relationships

We have to focus on our relationship to get the best return in life and improve our condition of being the victim of anger issues. I have come across many people suffering from relationship issues either with their parents or spouses. It becomes reflected in their behavior.

Studies show that 58% of human behavior is directly influenced by the environment in which the person grows and lives. This means that your home is the biggest influence in your life and a where you are spending most of your time. Therefore, it will have the greatest impact on your performance and behavior.

Sometimes, we think that relationship issues can cause colossal damage, a high stress level and mental illnesses like depression and excess anger. It is always advisable to spend time improving your relationships because they play a very prominent role in shaping your life.

Anger management is not a big issue if you can control your environment and the people in it, including your friends, colleagues, and spouse. The anger problem by getting the help of a professional or using the right information and advice.

In difficult situations, we have to think more logically and rationally. It helps to visualize the impact of our actions on our lives and that of others. Anger and a short temper can be brutal in one's professional life; it can destroy credibility and trust so it must be gotten rid of as soon as possible lest it become a curse.

Initially, it might be very difficult to get control of yourself and your emotions; but after following the techniques outlined in this book like taking a breath, remaining silent, effective communication skills, stretching, good sleep, and taking time out, major changes will come your way.

Keeping diary is also very helpful as it can serve as a gauge for to analyze your behavior after some time. This behavior impacts our loved ones, such as friends and family; so as soon we will realize what we are compromising, a new wonderful you will emerge.

Notes

____
____
____
____
____
____
____
____
____
____
____
____
____